REALLY EASY GUITAR

BILLIE EILISH

14 SONGS WITH CHORDS, LYRICS & BASIC TAB

T0087033

Cover photo by Frazer Harrison/Getty Images for Spotify

ISBN 978-1-5400-9393-6

Visit Hal Leonard Online at
www.halleonard.com

Contact us:
Hal Leonard
7777 West Bluemound Road
Milwaukee, WI 53213
Email: info@halleonard.com

In Europe, contact:
Hal Leonard Europe Limited
42 Wigmore Street
Marylebone, London, W1U 2RN
Email: info@halleonardeurope.com

In Australia, contact:
Hal Leonard Australia Pty. Ltd.
4 Lentara Court
Cheltenham, Victoria, 3192 Australia
Email: info@halleonard.com.au

GUITAR NOTATION LEGEND

Chord Diagrams

CHORD DIAGRAMS graphically represent the guitar fretboard to show correct chord fingerings.
- The letter above the diagram tells the name of the chord.
- The top, bold horizontal line represents the nut of the guitar. Each thin horizontal line represents a fret. Each vertical line represents a string; the low E string is on the far left and the high E string is on the far right.
- A dot shows where to put your fret-hand finger and the number at the bottom of the diagram tells which finger to use.
- The "O" above the string means play it open, while an "X" means don't play the string.

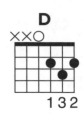

Tablature

TABLATURE graphically represents the guitar fingerboard. Each horizontal line represents a string, and each number represents a fret.

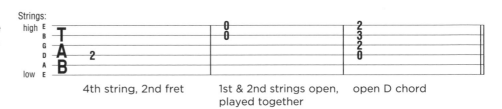

4th string, 2nd fret   1st & 2nd strings open, played together   open D chord

Definitions for Special Guitar Notation

HAMMER-ON: Strike the first (lower) note with one finger, then sound the higher note (on the same string) with another finger by fretting it without picking.

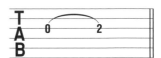

PULL-OFF: Place both fingers on the notes to be sounded. Strike the first note and without picking, pull the finger off to sound the second (lower) note.

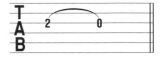

LEGATO SLIDE: Strike the first note and then slide the same fret-hand finger up or down to the second note. The second note is not struck.

SHIFT SLIDE: Same as legato slide, except the second note is struck.

Additional Musical Definitions

N.C.   • No chord. Instrument is silent.

   • Repeat measures between signs.

All the Good Girls Go to Hell

Words and Music by Billie Eilish O'Connell and Finneas O'Connell

(Capo 4th Fret)

B7	Em	C	Am
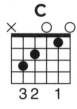		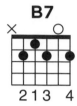	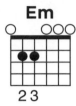

INTRO

Moderately

N.C.   B7
     My Lucifer is lonely.

VERSE 1

Em   C
    Standing there killing time,   can't commit to anything but a crime.

Am   B7
Peter's on vacation, an open invitation.

Em   C
    Animals, evidence.   Pearly gates look more like a picket fence.

Am   B7
 Once you get inside 'em, got friends, but can't invite them.

Em   C
    Hills burn in California.   My turn to ignore you.

Am   B7
    Don't say I didn't warn you.

CHORUS 1

Em   C   Am   B7
    All the good girls go to hell,   'cause even God herself   has enemies.

     Em   C   Am   B7
And once the waters start to rise   and heaven's out of sight,   she'll want the devil on her team.

Em C   Am   B7
    My Lucifer is lonely.

VERSE 2

Em   **C**
Look at you needing me.   You know I'm not your friend without some greenery.

Am   **B7**
Walk in wearing fetters. Peter should know better.

Em   **C**
Your coverup is caving in.   Man is such a fool; why are we saving him?

Am   **B7**
Poisoning themselves now, begging for our help. Wow.

Em   **C**
Hills burn in California.   My turn to ignore you.

Am   **B7**
Don't say I didn't warn you.

CHORUS 2

Em   **C**   **Am**   **B7**
All the good girls go to hell,   'cause even God herself   has enemies.

       Em   **C**   **Am**   **B7**
And once the waters start to rise   and heaven's out of sight,   she'll want the devil on her team.

Em   **C**   **Am**   **B7**
      My Lucifer is lonely.   (There's nothing left to say

Em   **C**   **Am**   **B7**
now.)   My God is gonna owe me.   (There's nothing left to say

Em   **C**   **Am**   **B7**   **Em**
now.)

Bad Guy

Words and Music by Billie Eilish O'Connell and Finneas O'Connell

Am
Dm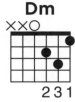
E7

INTRO

Moderately fast

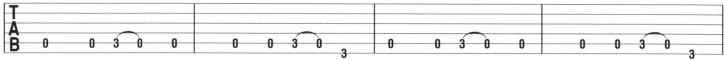

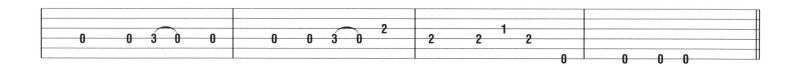

VERSE 1

Am
White shirt now red: my bloody nose. Sleeping. You're on your tippy toes,

Dm   **E7**
creeping around like no one knows. Think you're so criminal.

Am
Bruises on both my knees for you. Don't say thank you or please.

Dm   **E7**
I do what I want, when I'm wanting to. My soul, so cynical.

CHORUS 1

              Am
So you're a tough guy, "I like it really rough" guy,

"I just can't get enough" guy, "chest always so puffed" guy.

        Dm   **E7**
I'm that bad type, "make your mama sad" type, "make your girlfriend mad" type,

                          N.C.
"might seduce your dad" type.   I'm the bad guy.   Duh.

REPEAT INTRO

VERSE 2

N.C.(Am)
I like it when you take control. Even if you know that you don't

                             (E7)
own me, I'll let you play the role: I'll be your animal.

Am
My mommy likes to sing along with me, but she won't sing this song.

Dm   **E7**
If she reads all the lyrics, she'll pity the men I know.

REPEAT CHORUS

REPEAT INTRO

I'm on-ly good at be-ing

bad,   bad.

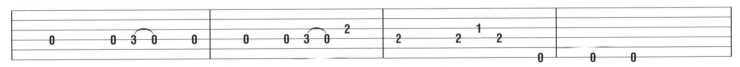

OUTRO

Half-time feel
Am
Spoken: I like when you get mad. I guess I'm pretty glad that you're alone.

You said she's scared of me. I mean, I don't see what she sees,

but maybe it's cause I'm wearing your cologne.

I'm the bad guy. Ha! I'm, I'm the bad guy, bad guy. Ha!

Bellyache

Words and Music by Billie Eilish and Finneas O'Connell

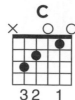

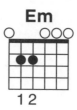

INTRO

Moderately

C Am Em
Mind,   mind.

C | Am | Em | ||

VERSE 1

C   Am   Em
Sitting all alone, mouth full of gum in the driveway.

  C   Am   Em
My friends aren't far, in the back of my car lay their bodies.

    C Am Em
Where's my mind? Where's my mind?

VERSE 2

   C   Am   Em
They'll be here pretty soon, looking through my room for the money.

   C   Am   Em
I'm biting my nails. I'm too young to go to jail; it's kind of funny.

    C Am Em
Where's my mind? Where's my mind?

    C Am Em
Where's my mind? Where's my mind?

CHORUS 1

              C   Am   Em

Maybe it's in the gutter where I left my lover. What an expensive   fate.

              C   Am   Em

My V is for Vendetta. Thought that I'd feel better and now I've got a bellyache.

VERSE 3

C   Am   Em

Everything I do, the way I wear my noose like a necklace.

 C   Am   Em

I wanna make them scared, like I could be anywhere, like I'm reckless.

        C   Am   Em

I lost my mind.   I don't mind.

            C   Am   Em

Where's my mind?   Where's my mind?

CHORUS 2

              C   Am   Em

Maybe it's in the gutter where I left my lover. What an expensive   fate.

              C   Am   Em

My V is for Vendetta. Thought that I'd feel better and now I've got a bellyache.

              C   Am   Em

Maybe it's in the gutter where I left my lover. What an expensive   fate.

              C   Am   N.C.

My V is for Vendetta. Thought that I'd feel better and now I've got a bellyache.

Bury a Friend

Words and Music by Billie Eilish O'Connell and Finneas O'Connell

(Capo 3rd Fret)

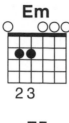  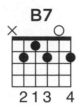

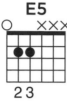  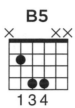

INTRO

Moderately

Billie.

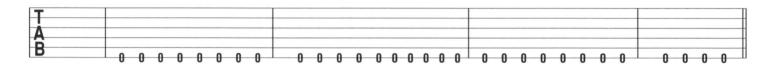

VERSE 1

N.C.   Em   Am
What do you want from me? Why don't you run from me?

B7   Em
What are you wondering? What do you know?

Am
Why aren't you scared of me? Why do you care for me?

B7   Em
When we all fall asleep, where do we go?

PRE-CHORUS 1

N.C.
(Come here.)

Em
Say it, spit it out. What is it exactly?

You're paying. Is the amount cleaning you out? Am I satisfactory?

Today I'm thinking about the things that are deadly.

The way I'm drinking you down, like I wanna drown, like I wanna end me.

CHORUS 1

E5   A5   B5   E5
    Step on the glass. Staple your tongue. (Ah.)   Bury a friend. Try to wake up. (Ah.)

E5   A5   B5   N.C.
    Cannibal class, killing the son. (Ah.)   Bury a friend.   I wanna end me.

E5   N.C.   E5   N.C.
                    I wanna end me.

Em
    I wanna, I wanna, I wanna end me. I wanna, I wanna, I wanna.

REPEAT VERSE 1

PRE-CHORUS 2

N.C.
    (Listen.)

Em
    Keep you in the dark. What had you expected:

    me to make you my art and make you a star and get you connected?

    I'll meet you in the park; I'll be calm and collected.

    But we knew right from the start that you'd fall apart, 'cause I'm too expensive.

    It's probably something that shouldn't be said out loud.

    Honestly, I thought that I would be dead by now. (Wow.)

    Calling security, keeping my head held down.

    Bury the hatchet or bury a friend right now.

BRIDGE

E5   A5   B5   E5
    For the debt I owe, gotta sell my soul, 'cause I can't say no. No, I can't say no.

                                    A5   B5   E5   N.C.
    Then my limbs are froze, and my eyes won't close, and I can't say no, I can't say no. (Careful.)

REPEAT CHORUS 1

REPEAT VERSE 1

Everything I Wanted

Words and Music by Billie Eilish O'Connell and Finneas O'Connell

Dmaj7 E C#m C#7

INTRO

Moderately fast

‖: Dmaj7   E | | C#m   Dmaj7 | :‖

VERSE 1

Dmaj7 E   C#m   Dmaj7
I had a dream   I got everything I wanted.

E   C#m   Dmaj7
Not what you'd think,   and if I'm being honest, it might have been a

E   C#m   Dmaj7
nightmare   to anyone who might care.

E   C#m   Dmaj7
Thought I could fly,   so I stepped off the Golden, mm.

E   C#m   Dmaj7
Nobody cried,   nobody even noticed. I saw them standing

E   C#m   Dmaj7
right there,   kind of thought they might care.

E   C#m   Dmaj7
I had a dream   I got everything I wanted.

E   C#m   Dmaj7
But when I wake up, I see you with me.

CHORUS 1

Dmaj7   E   C#m   Dmaj7
And you say, "As long as I'm here,   no one can hurt you.

E   C#m   Dmaj7
Don't want to lie here,   but you can learn to.

E   C#7   Dmaj7
If I could change the way   that you   see yourself,

E   C#m   Dmaj7
you wouldn't wonder why you're here.   They don't deserve you."

VERSE 2

Dmaj7   **E**   **C♯m**   **Dmaj7**
I tried to scream,   but my head was underwater.

            E   **C♯m**   **Dmaj7**
They called me weak,   like I'm not just somebody's daughter. It could have been a

     E   **C♯m**   **Dmaj7**
nightmare   but it felt like they were right there.

            E   **C♯m**   **Dmaj7**
And it feels like yesterday was a year ago, but I don't want to let anybody know.

            E   **C♯m**   **Dmaj7**
'Cause everybody wants something from me now, and I don't want to let them down.

  E   **C♯m**   **Dmaj7**
I had a dream   I got everything I wanted.

       E   **C♯m**   **Dmaj7**
But when I wake up, I see you with me.

REPEAT CHORUS 1

OUTRO

Dmaj7   **E**   **C♯m**   **Dmaj7**
If I knew it all then, would I do it again,   would I do it again?

          E   **C♯m**   **Dmaj7**
If they knew what they said would it go straight to my head,   what would they say instead?

        E   **C♯7**   **Dmaj7**
If I knew it all then, would I do it again,   would I do it again?

        E   **C♯m**   **Dmaj7**
If they knew what they said would it go straight to my head,   what would they say instead?

     E   **C♯m**   **Dmaj7**

Hostage

Words and Music by Billie Eilish and Finneas O'Connell

Am 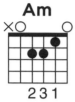 **C** 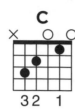 **Fmaj7** 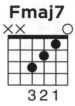 **E7** 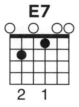 **Dm**

VERSE 1

Slow

Am   C   Fmaj7   Am   C   Fmaj7
I want to be alone.   Alone with you, does that make sense?

Am   C   Fmaj7   Am   C   Fmaj7
I want to steal your soul   and hide you in my treasure chest.

Am   C   Fmaj7 Am   C   Fmaj7
I don't know what to do,   to do with your kiss on my neck.

Am   C   Fmaj7   Am   C   Fmaj7
I don't know what feels true,   but this feels right so stay a sec.

       Am   C   Fmaj7
Yeah, you feel right, so stay a sec.

CHORUS 1

         E7   Fmaj7
And let me crawl inside your veins.

         E7   Fmaj7
I'll build a wall, give you a ball and chain.

         Dm   Fmaj7
I's not like me to be so mean, you're all I wanted.

         Dm   Fmaj7   Am   C   Fmaj7   Am   C Fmaj7
Just let me hold   you like a hostage.

VERSE 2

Am   C   Fmaj7 Am   C   Fmaj7
Gold on your fingertips,   fingertips against my cheek.

Am   C   Fmaj7 Am   C   Fmaj7
Gold leaf across your lips,   kiss me until I can't speak.

Am   C   Fmaj7   Am   C   Fmaj7
Gold chain beneath your shirt,   the shirt that you let me wear home.

Am   C   Fmaj7   Am   C   Fmaj7
Gold's fake and real love hurts and nothing hurts when I'm alone.

       Am   C   Fmaj7
When you're with me and we're alone.

CHORUS 2

        E7   Fmaj7
And let me crawl inside your veins.

        E7   Fmaj7
I'll build a wall, give you a ball and chain.

        Dm   Fmaj7
I's not like me to be so mean, you're all I wanted.

        Dm   Fmaj7
Just let me hold   you.

Dm   Fmaj7   Am   C   Fmaj7   Am   C   Fmaj7
Hold   you like a hostage.   Like a hostage.

Am   C   Fmaj7   Am   C   Fmaj7

I Love You

Words and Music by Billie Eilish O'Connell and Finneas O'Connell

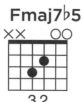 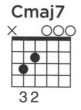 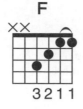 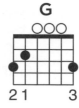 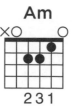

Fmaj7♭5   Cmaj7   F   G   Am

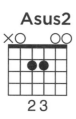 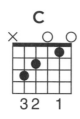 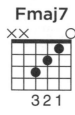  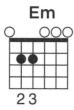

Asus2   C   Fmaj7   Dm   Em

INTRO

Moderately

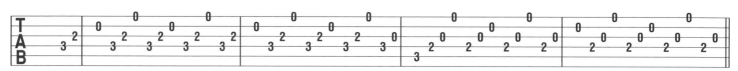

VERSE 1

    Fmaj7♭5   Cmaj7
It's not true. Tell me I've been lied to.

          Fmaj7♭5   Cmaj7
Crying isn't like you. Ooh.

              Fmaj7♭5   Cmaj7
What the hell did I   do? Never been the type   to

            Fmaj7♭5   Cmaj7
let someone see right through. Ooh.   Mm, hmm, mm, hmm.

CHORUS 1

F
Maybe, won't you take it back, say you were trying to make me laugh;

   G

and nothing has to change today: you didn't mean to say,

     Am   Asus2   C   Cmaj7
"I love you."   I love you,

            Fmaj7   Fmaj7♭5   Cmaj7
and I don't want to.   Ooh.

VERSE 2

Fmaj7♭5   Cmaj7
Up all night on another redeye.

      Fmaj7♭5   Cmaj7
I wish we'd never learned to fly, I.

       Fmaj7♭5   Cmaj7
Maybe we should just   try to tell ourselves a good lie.

      Fmaj7♭5   Cmaj7
Didn't mean to make you cry, I.   Mm, hmm, mm, hmm.

REPEAT CHORUS 1

BRIDGE

    Dm   Em   Fmaj7
The smile that you gave me, even when you felt like dying...

OUTRO/CHORUS

    F
We fall apart as it gets dark. I'm in your arms in Central Park.

     G
There's nothing you could do or say. I can't escape the way

    Am   Cmaj7
I love you.   I don't want to,

      Fmaj7♭5   Cmaj7
but I love you.   Ooh.

    Fmaj7♭5   Cmaj7
Ooh.   Ooh.

    Fmaj7♭5
Ooh.   Ooh.

idontwannabeyouanymore

Words and Music by Billie Eilish O'Connell and Finneas O'Connell

Cmaj7  **Gmaj7** 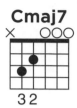 **Am7**  **D**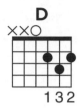

B7 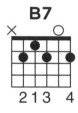 **C** 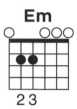 **Em**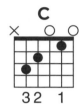

INTRO

Slow
Cmaj7   Gmaj7

        Am7   **Gmaj7**
By-di-da-die-da. By-di-da-die - da.

VERSE 1

Cmaj7   **Gmaj7**
Don't be that way, fall apart twice a day.

       Am7   **Gmaj7**
I just wish you could feel what you   say.

Cmaj7   **Gmaj7**
Show, never tell; but I know you too well,

       Am7   **D**
kind of mood that you wish you could   sell.

CHORUS 1

    Cmaj7   **Gmaj7**
If teardrops could be bottled, there'd be swimming pools filled by models

      Am7   **B7**
told a tight dress is what makes you a whore.

    Cmaj7   **Gmaj7**
If "I love you" was a promise, would you break it if you're honest,

      Am7   **D**
tell the mirror what you know she's heard before?

C   **B7**   **Em**
I don't wanna be you anymore.

VERSE 2

Cmaj7   Gmaj7
Hands getting cold, losing feeling is getting old.

   Am7   Gmaj7
Was I made from a broken   mold?

Cmaj7   Gmaj7
Hurt I can't shake, we've made every mistake.

   Am7   D
Only you know the way that I break, uh.

CHORUS 2

 Cmaj7   Gmaj7
If teardrops could be bottled, there'd be swimming pools filled by models

   Am7   B7
told a tight dress is what makes you a whore.

   Cmaj7   Gmaj7
If "I love you" was a promise, would you break it if you're honest,

   Am7   D
tell the mirror what you know she's heard before?

C   B7
I don't wanna be you,

C   B7
I don't wanna be you,

C   B7   Em
I don't wanna be you anymore.

Lovely

Words and Music by Billie Eilish O'Connell, Finneas O'Connell and Khalid Robinson

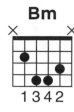
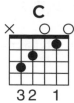

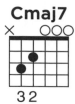

INTRO

Moderately

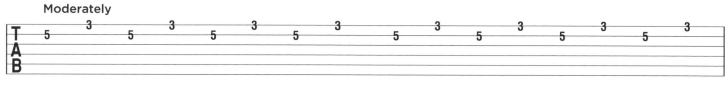

| Cmaj7 | | Em | Bm | |

| C | | Em | Bm | |

VERSE 1

C   Em   Bm
Thought I found a way, thought I found a way out.

      C   Em   Bm
But you never go away, so I guess I gotta stay now.

PRE-CHORUS

      Cmaj7   Em   Bm
Oh, I hope someday I'll make it out of here,

      Cmaj7   Em   Bm
even if it takes all night or a hundred years.

      Cmaj7   Em   Bm
Need a place to hide, but I can't find one near.

      Cmaj7   Em   Bm
Wanna feel alive, outside I can't fight my fear.

CHORUS 1

Cmaj7   Em   Bm
Isn't it lovely, all alone? Heart made of glass, my mind of stone.

Cmaj7   Em   Bm   C
Tear me to pieces, skin to bone.   Hello, welcome home.

VERSE 2

C   Em   Bm
Walking out of time, looking for a better place.

C   Em   Bm
Something's on my mind, always in my head space.

REPEAT PRE-CHORUS

CHORUS 2

Cmaj7   Em   Bm
Isn't it lovely, all alone? Heart made of glass, my mind of stone.

Cmaj7   Em   Bm
Tear me to pieces, skin to bone.   Hello, welcome home.

OUTRO

Cmaj7   Em   Bm
    Oh,   yeah.

C   Em Bm
Yeah, ah.   Oh, oh.

Cmaj7   Em   Bm

Cmaj7   Em   Bm   C
    Hello, welcome home.

No Time to Die

from NO TIME TO DIE

Words and Music by Billie Eilish O'Connell and Finneas O'Connell

Em 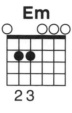 **Cmaj7** 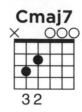 **A7** 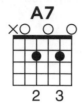 **B7**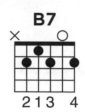

C  **A** 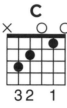 **Am**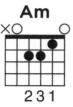

INTRO

Moderately

‖: Em | Cmaj7 | A7 | B7 :‖

VERSE 1

Em C   A   Am
I should have known

Em   C   A   Am
I'd leave alone.

Em   C   A   Am
Just goes to show

           C   B7
that the blood you bleed is just the blood you own.

Em   C   A   Am
We were a pair

Em   C   A   Am
but I saw you there,

Em   C   A   Am
too much to bear.

           C   B7
You were my life, but life is far away from fair.

PRE-CHORUS

     C   Em   Am   B7
Was I stupid to love you? Was I reckless to help? Was it obvious to everybody else

CHORUS 1

       Em   C Am
that I'd fallen for a lie?

       Em   C   Am
You were never on my side.

       Em   C   Am
Fool me once, fool me twice. Are you death or paradise?

       Em C   Am
Now you'll never see me cry.   There's just no time to die.

INTERLUDE

Em |Cmaj7 |A7 |B7 ||

VERSE 2

Em C   A   Am
  I let it burn

Em   C   A   Am
  that you're no longer my concern.

Em   C   A   Am
  Faces from my past return,

    C   B7
another lesson yet to learn,

REPEAT CHORUS

OUTRO

Em C   A7   B7
  No time to die.   Mm.

      Em   C A7   B7
No time to die.   Mm.

      Em   C   Am
Fool me once, fool me twice. Are you death or paradise?

      Em C   Am   Em
Now you'll never see me cry.   There's just no time to die.

Ocean Eyes

Words and Music by Finneas O'Connell

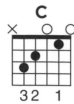 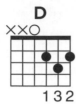 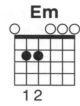 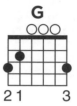

INTRO

Moderately

C   D   Em   C   D   Em
Ahh,   ahh,

C   D   Em   G   C
ahh,   ahh.

VERSE 1

C   D   Em   C   D   Em
I've been watching you for sometime.

C   D   Em   G   C
Can't stop staring at those ocean eyes.

C   D   Em   C D   Em
Burning cities and napalm skies.

C D   Em   G   C   G   C
Fifteen flares inside those ocean eyes, your ocean eyes.

CHORUS

        C D Em   C D Em
No fair.

         C   D   Em   G   C
You really know how to make me cry when you give me those ocean eyes.

         C D Em   C D Em
I'm scared.

         C   D   Em   G   C   G   C
I've never fallen from quite this high. Falling into your ocean eyes, those ocean eyes.

VERSE 2

C   D   Em   C   D   Em
I've been walking through a world gone blind.

C   D   Em   G   C
Can't stop thinking of your diamond mine.

C   D   Em   C   D   Em
Careful creature made friends with time.

     C   D   Em   G   C   G   C
He left her lonely with a diamond mine and those ocean eyes.

REPEAT CHORUS

INTERLUDE

‖: C   D   Em | C   D   Em |

C   D   Em | G   C   :‖ G   C   ‖

REPEAT CHORUS

Six Feet Under

Words and Music by Finneas O'Connell

 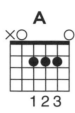 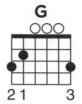   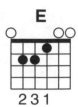

VERSE

Moderately

```
Bm    A    G    A     Bm A    G
```
Help; I lost myself again, but I   remember you.

```
Bm      A     G    A     Bm    A    G
```
Don't come back: it won't end well, but I wish you'd tell me to.

CHORUS 1

```
          Bm   A         Gmaj7 A
```
Our love is six feet under. I can't help but wonder:

```
          Bm   A         Em
```
if our grave was watered by the rain,

```
          G    A  Bm
```
would roses bloom?

```
          G    A  Bm   A Gmaj7
```
could roses bloom   again?

VERSE 2

```
    Bm   A   G    A     Bm   A    G
```
Retrace my lips. Erase your touch. It's all too much for me.

```
Bm   A    G    A      Bm   A    G
```
Blow away like smoke in air. How can you die carelessly?

CHORUS 2

        Bm   **A**   **Gmaj7** **A**
Our love is six feet under. I can't help but wonder:

        Bm   **A**   **Em**
if our grave was watered by the rain,

          G   **A** **Bm**
would roses bloom?

          G   **A** **Bm**   **A**
could roses bloom?

BRIDGE

          G   **A**   **Bm**
They're playing our sound, laying us down tonight.

      G   **A**   **Bm** **A**   **G**
And all of these clouds crying us back to life,   but you're cold as the night.

CHORUS 3

Bm   **A**   **G**   **A**
Six feet under. I can't help but wonder:

        Bm   **A**   **Em**
if our grave was watered by the rain...

G **A** **Bm**   **G**   **A** **Bm** **A** **Gmaj7**
Bloom.   Bloom   again.

OUTRO

Bm **A**   **G**   **A**   **Bm A**   **G**
Help; I lost myself again, but I   remember you.

When the Party's Over

Words and Music by Finneas O'Connell

(Capo 2nd Fret)

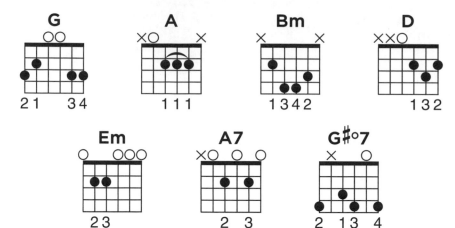

INTRO

Moderately

‖: G   A | Bm   A | D   A | G | | :‖
Mm.

VERSE 1

G   A Bm A D A   G
Don't you know I'm no good for you?

　　G　　A Bm A D   A   G
I've learned to lose you, can't af - ford to.

G   A Bm A D   A   G
Tore my shirt to stop you bleeding.

　　G　　A Bm A D　　A   G
But noth - ing ev - er stops you leaving.

N.C. (G)　　　　　　Bm　A   D   G
Quiet when I'm coming home, I'm on my own.

CHORUS 1

Em　　　　　Bm　　　　D　　　　　G
I could lie, say I like it like that, like it like that.

Em　　　　　Bm　　　　D　　　　　G
I could lie, say I like it like that, like it like that.

VERSE 2

G   A   Bm   A   D   A   G
Don't you know too much al - ready?

    G   A Bm A DA   G
I'll on - ly hurt you if you let me.

G   A Bm   A D   A   G
Call me friend, but keep me closer. (Call me back.)

     G A Bm   A D   A   G
And I'll call you when the par - ty's over.

G   A   Bm   A D A G
Quiet when I'm coming home, I'm on my own.

CHORUS 2

    Em   Bm   D   G
And I could lie, say I like it like that, like it like that.

    Em   Bm   D   G
Yeah, I could lie, say I like it like that, like it like that.

    Em   Bm   D   G
But nothing is better sometimes.

Em   Bm   D   G
Once we've both said our goodbyes,

A7   G   G#°7
let's just let it go.

   A7   G
And let me let you   go.

OUTRO

G   Bm   D   G
Quiet when I'm coming home, I'm on my own.

Em   Bm   D   G
I could lie, say I like it like that, like it like that.

Em   Bm   D   G
I could lie, say I like it like that, like it like that.

Wish You Were Gay

Words and Music by Billie Eilish O'Connell and Finneas O'Connell

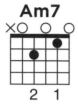
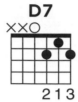
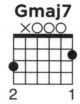

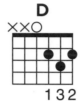
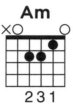

VERSE 1

Slow

     Am7   D7   Gmaj7   Em
"Baby, I don't feel so good," six words you never understood.

     Am7   D7   Gmaj7 Em
"I'll never let you go," five words you'll never say.

     Am7   D7   Gmaj7   Em
I laugh alone like nothing's wrong, four days has never felt so long.

     Am7   D7   G
If three's a crowd and two was us,   one slipped away.

CHORUS 1

Am7   D7   Gmaj7 Em
I just wanna make you feel okay,

   Am7   D7   Gmaj7   Em
but all you do is look the other way, mm.

Am7   D7   Gmaj7   Em
I can't tell you how much I wish I didn't wanna stay, mm.

Am7   D7   G
I just kinda wish you were gay.

VERSE 2

Am7   D7   Gmaj7   Em
Is there a reason we're not through? Is there a twelve-step just for you?

Am7   D7   Gmaj7 Em
Our conversation's all in blue, eleven "heys."

Am7   D7   Gmaj7   Em
Ten fingers tearing out my hair, nine time you never made it there.

Am7   D7   G
I ate alone at seven, you were six minutes away.

CHORUS 2

N.C.   Gmaj7   Em
How am I supposed to make you feel okay

Am7   D7   Gmaj7   Em
when all you do is walk the other way? Oh.

Am7   D7   Gmaj7   Em
I can't tell you how much I wish I didn't wanna stay, oh.

Am7   D7   G
I just kinda wish you were gay.

BRIDGE

Am7 D7   Gmaj7   Em
To spare my pride,   to give your lack of int'rest an explanation,

Am7 D7   Gmaj7   Em
Don't say I'm not your type.   Just say I'm not you preferred sexual orientation.

N.C. D7   Gmaj7   Em
I'm so selfish,   but you make me feel helpless, yeah.

Am7   D7
And I can't stand another day, stand another day.

OUTRO-CHORUS

Am7   D7   Gmaj7
I just wanna make you feel okay,

Am7   D7   Gmaj7
but all you do is look the other way, mm.

Am7   D7   Gmaj7   Em
I can't tell you how much I wish I didn't wanna stay, oh.

Am7   D7   G   Em
I just kinda wish you were gay.

Am7   D7   G   Em
I just kinda wish you were gay.

Am7   D7   G
I just kinda wish you were gay.

REALLY EASY GUITAR

Easy-to-follow charts to get you playing right away are presented in these collections of arrangements in chords, lyrics and basic tab for all guitarists.

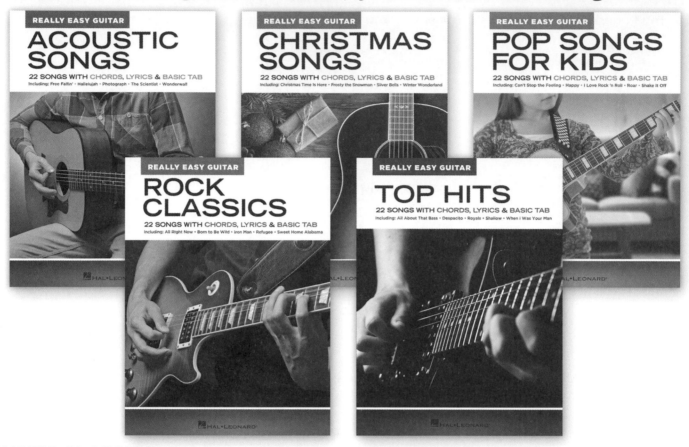

ACOUSTIC CLASSICS
22 songs: Angie • Best of My Love • Dust in the Wind • Fire and Rain • A Horse with No Name • Layla • More Than a Feeling • Night Moves • Patience • Time in a Bottle • Wanted Dead or Alive • and more.
00300600 ....$9.99

ACOUSTIC SONGS
22 songs: Free Fallin' • Good Riddance (Time of Your Life) • Hallelujah • I'm Yours • Losing My Religion • Mr. Jones • Photograph • Riptide • The Scientist • Wonderwall • and more.
00286663 ....$9.99

THE BEATLES FOR KIDS
14 songs: All You Need Is Love • Blackbird • Good Day Sunshine • Here Comes the Sun • I Want to Hold Your Hand • Let It Be • With a Little Help from My Friends • Yellow Submarine • and more.
00346031...$9.99

CHRISTMAS CLASSICS
22 Christmas carols: Away in a Manger • Deck the Hall • It Came upon the Midnight Clear • Jingle Bells • Silent Night • The Twelve Days of Christmas • We Wish You a Merry Christmas • and more.
00348327...$9.99

CHRISTMAS SONGS
22 holiday favorites: Blue Christmas • Christmas Time Is Here • Frosty the Snowman • Have Yourself a Merry Little Christmas • Mary, Did You Know? • Silver Bells • Winter Wonderland • and more.
00294775 ....$9.99

THE DOORS
22 songs: Break on Through to the Other Side • Hello, I Love You (Won't You Tell Me Your Name?) • L.A. Woman • Light My Fire • Love Her Madly • People Are Strange • Riders on the Storm • Touch Me • and more.
00345890 ....$9.99

BILLIE EILISH
14 songs: All the Good Girls Go to Hell • Bad Guy • Everything I Wanted • Idontwannabeyouanymore • No Time to Die • Ocean Eyes • Six Feet Under • Wish You Were Gay • and more.
00346351 ....$9.99

POP SONGS FOR KIDS
22 songs: Brave • Can't Stop the Feeling • Happy • I Love Rock 'N Roll • Let It Go • Roar • Shake It Off • We Got the Beat • and more.
00286698 ....$9.99

ROCK CLASSICS
22 songs: All Right Now • Born to Be Wild • Don't Fear the Reaper • Hey Joe • Iron Man • Old Time Rock & Roll • Refugee • Sweet Home Alabama • You Shook Me All Night Long • and more.
00286699 ....$9.99

TOP HITS
22 hits: All About That Bass • All of Me • Despacito • Love Yourself • Royals • Say Something • Shallow • Someone like You • This Is Me • A Thousand Years • When I Was Your Man • and more.
00300599...$9.99

HAL•LEONARD®

halleonard.com

0420